CW00393265

Strategic Management Practices of Non Profit Organisations

A UK Case Study

By H Parrott

Dedication

This work was written predominantly during my pregnancy with my first child, and was submitted to my university for my MBA shortly before she arrived. With that said, it seems fitting that this should be dedicated to my little girl and my husband for putting up with me.

About the Author

I didn't go to university at the conventional time, straight from college, it wasn't something my teachers pushed at the time. There is a lot to be praised for the Conservative governments introduced Narrowing the Gap project, alas, this came too late to benefit me. That being said, I do a lot of reflective practice, and in hind sight, it was right that I didn't go to university then. I left college and went straight to work for a high street bank – nothing to do with my actual qualification. Still wet behind the ears, I started as most do at the bottom, but I was a natural people person and progressed well. I learned so much from my time at the bank, not just about money, finance, accounts, money laundering, fraud etc. but about the diversity of people, their strengths, weakness' and vulnerabilities. Money is a very emotive topic, and us Brits don't like talking about our money, so I was in a very privilege position to listen and learn. I also learned a lot about management and strategy – that was something the bank we very good at, training. They spent lots on training their staff to progress, and at the time I thought this was wonderful, again looking back, they needed to as they had such a high turnover of staff, it was easier to promote from within. During my time there, and the other places I have worked, volunteered, and supported since, I can honestly say that I learned the most from the negative. When things went wrong, crisis management, and bad managers – oh we have all come across them, they have had me in tears to the point that they have made me ill. I came out stronger and learned lots about how to NOT be like them, and how to work with them if they are my manager.

Note: If you currently have a bad manager, take notes, see it as a learning exercise like studding an animal in the wild. They won't be your manager forever if they are that awful, and you will learn a lot from them on the way.

Contents

1.0 Introduction

1.1 Research Background

Strategic management of Non Profit Organisations (NPOs) in the United Kingdom is increasingly becoming complex owing to unprecedented levels of technological advancements, greater pressures for accountability by funders and the public, as well as the greater diversity of stakeholders in an increasingly globalised world (Hecht and Ramsey 2002). Since the 2000s, the UK non-profit and charity sector has undergone rapid expansion in scale and scope. Such developments have, in turn, considerably affected how NPOs should be managed. For instance, it has prompted non-profit managers to consider developing a market mindset, whereby they emphasise ensuring competitive advantages and financial sustainability of their firms (Macedo and Pinho 2004; Othman *et al.* 2014). As Macedo and Pinho (2004) explained, non-profit managers have realised that the new missions for their organisations entail attempting to influence donors to donate, volunteers to engage in voluntary works, clients to be responsive, and employees to be client-friendly, accountable and transparent.

Research has shown that non-profit managers find it difficult to gain absolute control over the affairs and the environment in which their organisations operate in the twenty-first century (Hecht and Ramsey 2002; Holatova and Dolezalova, 2014). There appears to be a consensus among management and social researchers that adopting strategic management in these organisations can enable non-profit managers to adequately address, influence, and get ready for the complexity of demands of their operating and external environment (Holatova and Dolezalova, 2014). Some scholars have recommended the need to use formal-strategy formation processes - such as structured strategic planning model - owing to their potential to encourage transparent decision-making, and greater levels of accountability (Anheier 2000; Bryson 2004).

Compared to the management teams of organisations designed for a commercial purpose, which have pressures to achieve operational efficiency and financial prosperity, the management teams of NPOs are usually not experienced or skilled in strategic management practices (Othman *et al.* 2014). An underlying cause is that NPOs rely heavily on, and therefore culturally disproportionately value voluntary participation and amiability, and establishing informal relationships, which, in turn, alienates the notion of overt accountability. Such intrinsic attributes of NPOs have made them lose or reduce focus on management accounting and control practices, by choosing to divert resources of time and money elsewhere, provided that the social missions, values and aims are achieved. Such attributes are problematic for NPOs because of the changing operational environment (Hecht and Ramsey 2002). In the case of the United Kingdom, insufficiency and a lack of accounting information are causing NPOs to fail to benefit from financial sustainability, improvement and expansion, and to leverage the strategic skills for predicting failures and implementing advanced financial planning and control mechanism (Acevo 2017). While some commentators have reasoned that this is because of the lack of availability of resources and funding, some NPOs have underscored the need to implant the principle of accountability of their operations, as all organisations, despite their nature, must be answerable to their stakeholders.

It appears that NPOs in the UK have either failed or have been slow to adopt strategic management "best practices" (Acevo 2017). In turn, the management of these organisations has been exposed to uncertainty regarding how they can restructure strategic management practices of their organisations. This forms the basis of this research.

1.2 Research Problem

NPOs in the UK are evolving and adjusting to address various complex demands, including conforming to government requirements and pressures to be accountable and transparent in their financial management, responding to the changing external environment, and the demands of their beneficiaries. Similarly, they are confronted by greater levels of scrutiny from the public through social media platforms, the mainstream media, and funders, particularly after the fall of Kids Company - which revealed how some NPOs engage in inappropriate fundraising and mismanage funds (Acevo 2017).

The UK not for profit sector is a fundamental component of the UK social fabric, with an estimated 160,000 registered NPOs in England and Wales, and other community social groups and social enterprises. These organisations are encumbered by poor strategic management practices, leading to lack of stability of their incomes. For instance, NPOs with incomes ranging from £25,000 to £1 million tend to experience financial volatility, with nearly one-third of these NPOs being highly susceptible to external shocks due to bad management (Acevo 2017).

Some cases of NPO employee fraud, organisational mismanagement, and collapse have been noted in the UK. An example for this includes the collapse of a London youth work non-profit organisation Kids Company in 2015. The organisation was found to have collapsed as a result of financial management problems (Elgot, 2015). The organisation was overwhelmed by financial turmoil after the UK government cancelled its annual £5 million grant. It was later accused of lacking an efficient governance structure, inability to incorporate "best practices" in governance, employee fraud, and financial mismanagement (The Guardian, 2015).

Despite internal functioning problems (as opposed to financial problems) beginning to be appreciated by NPOs as drivers to internal control problems and management failures, they have received nominal attention, particularly in the UK. Additionally, NPOs with weak financial control mechanisms are likely to report internal control problems and management failures. There is a lack of research as regards the extent to which strategic management practices of NPOs in the UK vary from the management of conventional profit-making businesses, and how NPOs are adopting effective strategies to ensure their long-term financial and competitive sustainability (Holatova and Dolezalova, 2014; Macedo and Pinho, 2004; Othman et al., 2014).

1.3 Research Purpose

This research investigates the assumption that current management and organisational research have not adequately addressed the question of strategic management of NPOs in the UK, whether they should be managed distinctly from the profit-driven business firm, and whether they should be managed using different management practices and models. The study explored the strategic management practices of NPOs in the UK to determine their variation from the management of conventional profit-making businesses, and to determine how they can form effective strategies to ensure their long-term sustainability.

1.4 Research aims and objectives

The aim of the research is to explore the strategic management practices in NPOs operating in the UK.

The main study objectives include:

- Explore the strategic management practices used by NPOs in the UK;

- Investigate the strategic management models used by NPOs;

- Determine how strategic practices of NPOs differ from those of for-profit organisations;

- Examine the effects of NPO's external environmental and internal context on strategy formation processes;

- Investigate how Organisations in the UK respond to changes in the internal and external environment;

- Determine the reasons for strategic management choices made by NPOs in the UK.

1.5 Research Questions

Building on research aims and objectives, the proposed research questions include:

- What strategic management practices do NPOs in the UK use?

- What strategic models do NPOs in the UK use?

- In what ways do the strategic management practices of NPOs differ from those of for-profit organisations?

- How does UK NPO's external environmental and internal context and strategy formation processes influence the strategies they use?

- How do NPOs in the UK set up strategic management strategies to respond to changes in the internal and external environment?

- What reasons underlie the use of strategic management in NPOs in the UK?

1.6 Significance

Strategic management of NPOs is a complex and uncertain endeavour for NPO executives and boards of management. This study will contribute to knowledge on how poor strategic management can contribute to poor service delivery, collapse of NPOs, and how these can be avoided through appropriate strategic management practices. By proving an improved understanding of strategic management practices and their implications, the proposed study hopes that NPOs will be able to attain greater financial sustainability. This will also have a theoretical significance, as it will generate greater insights into the variation between management practices of NPOs and profit-making businesses to inform empirical research and organisational practices.

1.7 Theoretical Framework

The study draws on a resource dependant conceptual framework to explore the strategic management practices in NPOs. The resource-dependence theory hypothesises that an organisation's behaviour is influenced by the extent of its resource dependencies (Hillman *et al.*, 2009). It attempts to demonstrate that external factors will almost automatically influence organisational behaviour, and while organisations will be restricted by their contexts, their management teams can develop strategies to limit their vulnerability to environmental uncertainty and dependencies. Salancik and Pfeffe (1978) proposed the theory in their works "The External Control of Organisations: A Resource Dependence Perspective." To date, the theory has been applied as a framework for organisational theory and strategic management research. Pfeffer and Salancik (1978) argued that for organisations to survive, they require resources (such as capital, labour, legitimacy, and clientele) that external factors control. This then causes interdependencies that may contribute to an imbalance of power over who should control them. When these resources are scarce, the funders or suppliers of these resources have greater power, which may lead the organisation to lose autonomy and an ability to freely undertake managerial and strategic discretion as required (Pfeffer and Salancik, 1978).

NPO's revenue structure and management practices present an opportunity to understand the manner in which they behave and the management practices they adopt. Their fate also depends on the extent to which they can access resources (Verbruggen *et al.*, 2009). Using this assumption as a basis, it is reasoned that the specific type of resource dependence by NPOs in the UK may also explain the behaviours and the management practices they adopt. Previous studies have successfully applied the resource dependence framework to NPOs and have demonstrated that the theory provides an essential theoretical model for exploring problem assessments, perspectives, and strategies used by non-profit-making organisations (Macedo and Pinho, 2004).

1.8 Dissertation structure

Chapter one of this dissertation consists of the Introduction chapter, where research background on how NPOs in the UK have either failed to, or have been slow to adopt strategic management "best practices" is discussed. It also consists of:

- The research problem regarding how NPOs are likely to report an internal control problem and management failures.
- An outline of the research purpose, research aims and objectives, research questions and significance, and a discussion of the theoretical framework.

Chapter 2 consists of the literature review section: reviewing previous research on strategic management practices and models used by NPOs', strategic management practices and their variation from management of for-profit organisations, influence of NPOs' external and internal environmental context on strategy formation and use, the development of strategic plans in response to changes internal and external environment, and reasons for strategic management by NPOs.

Chapter 3 consists of the research methodology section, discussing the research philosophy used along with the research paradigm, the qualitative research methods, the approach used for the data collection method and sampling procedures, and a discussion on ethical considerations.

Chapter 4 consists of the data analysis section and discusses the research findings.

Chapter 5 consists of the discussion section and attempts to interpret and explain the implication of research findings in the reflection of what is already known regarding the research problems examined. It also describes new insights regarding the research problems.

Chapter 6 consists of the conclusion and recommendation section. Here, findings of the research are summarised to how they have contributed to research knowledge on strategic management practices of NPOs in the UK, their failures and recommendations.

2.0 Literature Review

2.1 Strategic management practices in NPOs

A NPO has been described as an organisation whose "predominantly non-business characteristics" influence its operations that are designed to carry out a social mission, create social value, or deliver public benefits, as opposed to generating profit (Othman *et al.*, 2014). In the last decade, the non-profit and charity sector has experienced rapid expansion in scope, which demonstrates their increased significance in the society. Such developments have affected how the NPOs are managed by prompting non-profit managers to develop a market mindset (Macedo and Pinho 2004; Othman *et al.* 2014). As Macedo and Pinho (2004) explained non-profit managers have realised that their new missions entail influencing donors to donate.

Related literature has demonstrated that a market-oriented mindset has advantages in terms of encouraging efficiency in profit-driven business firms. It encourages organisations to design the most suitable services to the target clients and can enable sustainable competitive advantage by encouraging organisations to create superior customer value and better organisational performance (Macedo and Pinho 2004; Othman *et al.* 2014). Macedo and Pinho (2004) argue that adopting resource-based strategies can enable NPOs to adopt a change of attitude with respect to obtaining and managing their funding sources and their management strategies. Put differently, NPOs must seek ways to efficiently manage their resources efficiently to improve their performance in an increasingly complex internal and external environment.

A relevant body of research exists that accounts for the basic dynamics linked to the environmental effect on organisations, and how they can react to environmental limitations to their management capacity. The assumption is built on the resource dependence theory, which contends that organisations can attain ultimate survival depending on their capacity to obtain and maintain resources (Pfeffer and Salancik, 1978, p. 2).

The origin of strategic management can be traced to the mid-1980s, which was marked by a growth rate of competition, increased pressures for innovation, and a rise in a tendency to be customer-oriented. The objective of management practices was to establish and understand strategies that would embody a competitive advantage (Holatova and Dolezalova, 2014). Similarly, organisations of non-profit sector started using principles of strategic management. Strategic management refers to a combination of managerial decisions and activities that can be applied in the facilitation of competitive advantage and long-term superior organisational performance. They focus on limiting organisational weaknesses and leveraging their strengths, and anticipating future problems and likely opportunities. Within the context of NPOs, Holatova and Dolezalova (2014) observed that strategic management is usually typified by diverse expectations and purposes of varied stakeholders, influencing donors, multi-source financing, and attracting grants from governments and sponsors. Previous studies that examined strategic management and organisational effectiveness mostly used mixed research and qualitative research methods.

A study by Herman and Renz (2004) used a qualitative research approach to investigate local NPO's effectiveness. They concentrated on two NPOs. The first was a health and welfare service provider that was funded by the local United Way, the second attended to developmentally disabled children, which surveyed 30 respondents. Their study established a relationship between the effectiveness of the board and the effectiveness of the organisation. There also appeared to be a consensus among respondents that an adjustment in the use of management practices was not linked to a shift in opinion regarding the overall effectiveness of the organisations.

In a related qualitative research study, Courtney *et al*. (2009) interviewed CEOs of NPOs to determine the strategic management approaches they used. The researchers collected data using interviews with housing NPOs. They categorised the organisations under "sophistication" and "approach." In the "approach" category, they developed a four-category typology building on the alternatives that the organisation can pursue growth. Under the sophistication category, they developed a three-category building on the tools and techniques the organisation applied in strategic planning. Their findings indicated a strong relationship between the size of the organisation and sophistication in strategic planning. While the larger sized firms indicated high-performance ratings, the smaller ones indicated lower performance.

Rehor *et al.* (2014) examined strategic management methods in NPOs. Based on systematic review of the literature, they revealed that NPOs tend to focus their strategic management practices towards solving problems identified in the external environment. Current literature has shown that the failure or success of NPOs is essentially contingent on strategic decision-making. Related literature has indicated that strategic management should make sure that organisational management did not occur randomly but based on clarified long-term objectives (Weerawardena and Mort, 2012). According to Weerawardena and Mort (2012), NPO leaders should be open to shifting goals and activities, with regards to changing situations in the external or internal environments. As a result, organisational leaders need to consistently monitor, evaluate, and benefit from constant feedback. It is on this basis that strategic management could be reasoned as a fluid, and ongoing approach, as opposed to a one-shot approach.

Rehor *et al.* (2014) contend that strategic management should also be considered as a process and a means of contemplating about aspects of an organisation, such as long- and short-term goals, stakeholders, and achieving efficiency. It is a continuous intricate process of management that agrees on the organisational targets and a strategic course for reaching specific targets. To this end, strategic management can be interpreted as a combination of management decisions and action plans that the management can employ to enable competitive advantage, and long-term better performance of an organisation. Consequently, it potentially reduces organisational weaknesses and leverages their strengths by anticipating prospects and problems.

Within the context of NPOs, strategic management is distinguished by diverse functions and expectations of different groups, impacts of donors, funding from multiple sources, and a high fraction of resources from sponsors. As a consequence, for successful strategic management of an organisation, the organisation has to be aware of issues regarding its reasons for its existence, changes in the needs and structures of the organisation over time, and whether it has adequate human and financial resources (Weerawardena et al., 2010).

Seemingly, the non-profit sector is attracting an increased volume of research to explore the basis of successful value creation, through strategic management. To advance non-profit sector research beyond its present emphasis on conceptualising the concept of strategic management. Weerawardena and Mort (2012) used multiple theoretical case studies to examine the competitive strategy in socially entrepreneurial NPOs. They established that focus on ensuring the sustainability of for-profit businesses has prevailed in the strategic management literature for many decades. This discovered that the market orientation discourse, the resource advantage theory, and the resource-based view, fundamentally reveal the necessity of for-profit organisations to achieve competitive advantages that enabled them to grow and survive over the long-term.

Despite this, the non-profit literature seems not to reveal that NPOs have emphasised attaining competitive advantages to enable them to grow and survive over the long-term, in spite of an increasing rate of threats to their sustainability (Mort and Weerawardena, 2008).

Innate dissimilarities between for-profit and NPOs may prevent the direct use of theories derived from the business sector. Fundamentally, NPOs diverge considerably from the for-profit organisations in numerous and considerable ways. For-profit organisations seek to persistently create greater shareholder wealth by delivering superior value to its customers. Alternatively, NPOs make efforts for financial resources to bring in social value to its stakeholders. Related literature on the NPOs operating environment indicate that these types of organisations operate in a highly complex and demanding multi-stakeholder environment and therefore require advanced strategic management processes (Kohli and Jaworski 1990).

2.2 Strategic Management Models used by NPOs

To determine the approaches that NPOs can use to develop their strategy, Courtney *et al.* (2009) used the term "sophistication" to define the strategic analysis, development, and implementation of strategic planning in organisations. The research interviewed CEOs and reviewed organisation to develop a three-level sophistication scale consisting of an informal planner, partial planners, and full planners. In a later study, Courtney *et al.* (2009) also employed the term strategic approach to refer to the rules that organisations use to determine their operation scope. The process inspired the creation of four strategic approach categories; all opportunistic expansionists; opportunists; incrementalists; and niche strategists.

Opportunistic expansionists organisations expand their scope of operations with time, outside their original mission to cover new geographical areas.

Opportunistic organisations expand their scope of operations outside their original mission to pursue innovation outside of their written plans and objectives.

Incrementalists are organisations that have previously demonstrated an interest in extending beyond their mission, yet have failed to capitalise on the existing opportunities to do so.

Niche strategists are organisations that stick to their missions and objectives and have not considered expanding beyond their niche.

The "market orientation" model and the "market-driven firm paradigm" are emphasised in for-profit literature, and reveal the importance placed on satisfying and retaining customers. Weerawardena *et al*. (2010) observed that NPOs must lay a comparatively lower emphasis on clients than on donors. Although focusing on clients has a potential to ensure better service delivery in NPOs, the link between the clients and generation of revenue is fundamentally detached in NPOs. According to Weerawardena *et al*. (2010), donors are placed at the centre owing to the decisive role they play in the provision of revenue stream, that is significant for the operation of an NPO. Also, governments and entrepreneurial business initiatives nested within the NPO have provided other important sources of finance for NPOs. Volatility across all these diverse revenue streams forces NPOs to become adept at multiple stakeholder management.

Weerawardena *et al*. (2010) also attempted to focus on 'balancing money and mission' as the principal concern in the management of NPOs. Some theoretical models and experiential comparisons have considered such constructs as production quality, pricing, production quantity, improvement of service quality, and budgeting practice. An NPO needs to make sure there is a flow of resources to ensure long-term sustainability (Valentinov, 2008). NPOs obtain funding through, governmental support, earned income and donation from private entities.

Scholars who have contributed to this body of literature tend to suggest numerous strategies that NPOs can espouse to boost their financial substantiality. These include revenues generated commercially, using business principles to strategic alliances, and application of relationship marketing (Valentinov 2008; Weerawardena *et al.* 2010). Besides the strategies for generating revenues, scholars have proposed some strategies that can be employed to cut costs. These include greater productivity, greater soliciting of volunteerism and requesting for in-kind donations.

In the last decade, some scholars have arrived at a consensus that 'earned income strategies' can be used to attain organisational sustainability, which integrates the attributes of non-profit with for-profit organisations (Peredo and McLean, 2006; Weerawardena *et al.* 2010). In a related study, Mair and Marti (2006) extended this perspective by arguing that 'social entrepreneurship may also be effectively applied on a for-profit basis'. Using case study qualitative research approach, Mair and Marti (2006) identified three 'social ventures' that have attempted this strategy. These include Grameen Bank in Bangladesh, Aravind Hospital in India, and Sekem Chemicals in Egypt.

The profits that these organisations generate from their principal activities are applied in engaging in numerous social ventures. For instance, Sekem in Egypt operates as a multi-business that has succeeded in reducing pesticides applied in cotton fields in Egypt by 90 percent. The organisation has developed learning institutions and a health centre (Seelos and Mair, 2005). Mair and Marti (2006) argued that 'the selection of the set-up is essentially directed by the types of the social needs tackled, the number of resources required, and the possibility of raising revenues'.

2.3 Strategic Management Practices of NPOs and their Variation from Management of for-profit Organisations

The principal–agency theory hypothesises that for-profit organisations are more efficient than NPOs as their managers aspire to increase shareholders' returns. On the other hand, non-profits ought to provide an enhanced quality of services through service to the community, provision of charity, undertaking pieces of research, and invitation of philanthropic supporters. This difference is not evenly supported across the non-profit literature. A blend of studies undertaken in the past two decades demonstrates disparities between for-profit and NPOs, yet the findings appear not to be conclusive and are somewhat conflicting in some cases (Reeves and Ford 2004).

Some studies have emphasised on differences in quality of care and profits. Costs and revenues affect the growth in equity and profits of organisations, in spite of how they are measured (Reeves and Ford 2004). The costs and revenues are revenues that must be taken into consideration in the assessment of measures that relate to them. According to Reeves and Ford (2004), NPOs tend to have lower levels of daily adjusted costs compared to for-profit organisations, such as those for Medicare psychiatric patients. The researchers showed that the rates for per capita Medicare spending and the rise in rates tended to be greater in areas dominated by for-profit organisations in comparison to those predominantly served by NPOs.

The cost categories tended to be higher for for-profit organisations than for NPOs that operated as hospitals even after adjustments for taxes as the costs for administration costs were relatively high. According to Ettner and Hermann (2001), patients in NPO hospitals tended to have longer stays for each admission, which suggested that they were relatively less efficient in their operations. Shukla and Clement established conflicting results. They found that patients tended to stay longer in for-profit hospitals, which also had smaller staff-to-patient ratios. Consistent with this finding, King and Avery established that in the process of conversion to other forms, for-profit hospitals tended to reduce the nurse-to-patient ratio after they acquired a non-profit hospital, cut redundant programs, did away with research and educational programs, and reduced community welfare and health initiatives. While they established very nominal dissimilarity, despite whether for-profit hospitals transformed to non-profit hospitals or non-profit hospitals transformed to for-profit ones, NPOs showed a remarkable tendency to boost staff-to-patient ratios once they acquired a for-profit based hospital.

In a related study, Mobley and Magnussen assessed long-term and short-term efficiency, which they portray as a rise in a single output that requires a reduction in a different output or arises in at least a single input — as was in the case of hospitals in California. In the long-term, the researchers established that the for-profit hospitals tended to have lower levels of group-wise efficiency compared to non-profit hospitals in urban California.

2.4 Influence of NPO's External and Internal Environmental Context on Strategy Formation and Use

Researchers have attempted to explain how NPOs external environmental and internal context and strategy formation processes influence how strategic management practices are implemented (Giffords and Dina, 2004). It appears that there is no real consensus on how this should happen. Some scholars like Giffords and Dina (2004) emphasised that NPOs rely on strategic planning to prioritise the strategies they use in their internal and external environments.

In their view, the main advantage of creating a strategic plan within the framework of continuous quality and performance improvement (CQPI) is to enable non-profit's management and employees to acclimatise the organisation to the existing internal and external environment, prioritise the organisation's mission, and illuminate client's needs (Hoonakkera *et al.* 2010). As Wilbur (2000) reveals, this ongoing process sustains the necessity for NPOs to continually improve quality services to their clients while revealing to their funders and other concerned stakeholders that the organisation has a positive effect on them.

Giffords and Dina (2004) define strategic planning as a systematic process that assists in bringing a consensus as regards organisational priorities among the primary stakeholders to assist an organisation to meet its mission (Wilbur, 2000). Within the context of NPOs, strategic planning is more complicated than planning in the for-profit organisations, whereby managers aim to increase shareholder's wealth. NPO's are concerned with the systematic management of external and internal environment factors. The base on which plans are built is through assessments of these environments. The external and internal environmental context influence the strategies that NPOs use.

While evaluating an NPO's internal environment, the managers may discover conflicting perspectives of the organisation's mission and vision, and degree of efficiency. Giffords and Dina (2004) expressed concern that individuals working in NPOs may find themselves becoming increasingly immersed in the everyday operation of the organisations, which may influence them to concentrate on "program ends rather than the purpose" that they are intended to accomplish. Organisational cultures and values should as well be taken into consideration as they directly affect the organisation's operation (Giffords and Dina, 2004). When the leadership of the organisation seeks to create a strategic plan, they need first to undertake an internal analysis to discover issues that potentially affect the organisation. Afterwards, they should endeavour to position those deemed vital within their organisations' context.

Steiner *et al.* (1994) identified internal indicators that enhance the urgency for planning, particularly in the increasingly aggressive non-profit environment. These include periods of stagnant organisational growth, administrative operations, and high employee turnover or changes in leadership. The external environment is also essential for the functioning of NPOs, particularly in periods where there is a high competition for limited funds, changes in client priorities, shifts in accreditation requirements, and societal changes (Giffords and Dina, 2004).

2.5 Developing a Strategic Plan in Response to changes Internal and External Environment

According to Giffords and Dina (2004), CQPI is a valuable tool that NPOs can use to adapt to the changing external and internal environments. Non-profit researchers like Pecora and Seelig (2001) support this assumption. Pecora and Seelig (2001) consider a CQPI plan as a systematic process for committing to the constituents of an organisation, pledging to advance all areas of operation persistently. Giffords and Dina (2004) view it as an organisation's pledge to its clients and the greater community to offer them efficient and effective services. This implies that the CQPI process is set up to build on evaluations of an organisation's performance and to execute targeted improvements rapidly.

Mikulas and Cohan (2001) made a similar conclusion, stressing that setting up a CQPI implies that the planning, goal-setting and attainment activities of an organisation are provided with information using a formal feedback process, including that of external assessments, to bring about improved performance that is beneficial to both the organisation and its constituents. The assessment should be accurate, as Giffords and Dina (2004) highlighted, having an accurate evaluation process is critical. This implies gathering accurate data regarding a problem and analysing and interpreting it empirically. In the end, an accurate evaluation process has a potential to help an organisation to obtain a comprehensible outlook of the future and to develop relevant goals. In the process of developing a strategic plan, organisations need to carefully decide whom to include in the planning process, including the board of directors, management staff, some employees, funders, members of the community, clients, and volunteers. Steiner *et al.* (1994) advised that implementation of the strategic plan should then follow once it is developed. The organisation's employees will need to take part in this process collectively.

2.6 Reasons for Strategic Management by NPOs

Many scholars agree that strategic planning helps NPOs to make informed decisions regarding their prospect (Ogonji 2014). In spite of the divergent opinion regarding the effectiveness of strategic planning, the models used should be able to generate reliable results to be acceptable (Mulhare, 1999). Although NPOs are supposed to be beneficial to the society at large, there are cases where the opposite happens. A study by Ogonji (2014) showed that a majority of volunteers tend to be uncertain of what the organisations look forward to getting from them. The researcher mentioned incidences of embezzlement of public funds and cases, where NPOs failed to live up to their stakeholders' expectations. According to Ogonji (2014), strategic planning enabled organisations to envisage the future and agree on what should be done to get there by adopting new approaches and developing a new shared vision. Similar results are reflected in Bryson's (2010) study, where they established that strategic management encourages strategic thinking and actions to respond to a situational issue in an organisation. It leads to a clarification of vision, assists organisations to discover best strategies, promotes consensus - building among stakeholders and improves the capacity of organisations to make a quality decision that reflects back to organisational objectives and mission.

Strategic management also becomes useful when organisations change their scope of operation or mission. A study by Bryson and Alsto (2011) indicated the challenges confronting NPOs that prompt them to set up strategic management. The researchers outlined that a rise in demand for services that NPOs offer, a greater level of competition, problems in the acquisition of funds, a desire to collaborate with other organisations, greater pressures for transparency and accountability, and increased levels of doubt regarding economic, political and social changes of the future, prompted NPOs to engage in strategic management. Ogonji (2014) validated these findings, and he centred on the contemporary problems confronting non-profits. They identified them as including income disparity between the poor and the rich, continually diminishing funding by the government, and increased pressures on NPOs to publish and explain results of their operation to donors, owing to the general belief that they allocate a huge proportion of their budgets on overheads. Additional triggers identified in Ogonji's (2014) research include higher levels competition and innovativeness from social enterprises.

3.0 Research Methodology

This chapter provides an overview of the varied alternatives open to the researcher prior to the start of data collection. The section provides a detail of the research approaches in research that are determined to be the most suitable for the topic. It also provides options that the researcher needs to make. It starts off with the research aims and objectives since the methodology must be in step with them. Afterward, the description of the approaches to be selected is also discussed, followed by the research method before ending with the data analysis.

3.1 Research Aims and Objectives

Research Aim: The aim of the research is to explore the strategic management practices in NPOs operating in the UK.

Research Objectives:

- Explore the strategic management practices used by NPOs in the UK;
- Investigate the strategic management models used by NPOs;
- Determine how strategic practices of NPOs differ from those of for-profit organisations;
- Examine the effects of NPO's external environmental and internal context on strategy formation processes;
- Investigate how Organisations in the UK respond to changes in the internal and external environment;
- Determine the reasons for strategic management by NPOs in the UK.

3.2 Research Approach

Using an interpretivist research approach is appropriate for subjective interpretation of reality. It makes sure that the reality can be wholly understood (Saunders *et al.* 2003). Consistent with the research objectives, the approach would consider non-profit managers as having a capacity to construct meanings depending on how they interpret strategic management practices in NPOs. The interpretivist philosophy is selected for the study, as it depends on inductive reasoning.

An inductive approach was also used in the research to help examine the emergent generalisations from non-profit managers' perspectives strategic management practices of NPOs in the UK. The approach was used to facilitate the formation of emergent generalisations. It was considered to be appropriate for the study, as known premises would be used in the process of generating untested conclusions regarding strategic management practices of NPOs (Williams, 2007).

3.2.1 Relevance of the Approach

An interpretivist research approach was considered to be appropriate for the study, owing to its capacity to facilitate a survey of research participants in their natural setting and that it acknowledged that the researcher does not affect the phenomena under study (Creswell, 2002). The study also used the approach, as it relates to how people attempt to make sense of their natural settings and to construct meanings attached to their experiences in their natural setting. The objectives of the proposed research fall within an interpretive approach as they require an exploration of the deep-seated meanings attached to strategic management practices in NPOs.

3.3 Research Design

Consistent with the inductive approach, a qualitative case study research design was used in the studies. A qualitative research design presents a systematic approach to studying the phenomenon in participants' natural setting and facilitate the development of research details from real experiences of the participants. A case study research is appropriate for explanatory and exploratory research and is suitable for confronting a specific organisational context. It is well adapted to explore complex organisational phenomena and this study relies on a qualitative case study. The non-profit sector is greatly heterogeneous and is characterised by a variety of organisations. It is 'an empirical inquiry designed for investigating a contemporary phenomenon within their real-life contexts, in cases where the boundaries between research phenomenon and their context are particularly distinct, and where the research seeks for numerous sources of evidence' (Yin 1984). Multiple case studies were used in this study as they are considered to be capable of providing robust research results than single case studies.

The case study method was used in the research as it permits the grouping of different sources of evidence from semi-structured interviews and document analysis (Mariotto *et al.* 2012). To highlight the needs underscored in the review of the literature, the proposed study will utilise a mixed-method comparative multi-case study of a group of NPOs with similar operations in the areas of service offering, client needs, funding needs, technological complexity and changing competitive dynamics. The participants were to be selected from the sampling frame of 10 organisations to be compiled in the UK. The research only managed to access seven organisations, as the other three NPOs turned down the interview on the grounds of privacy and confidentiality. The multi-case study facilitated an interview and analysis of the strategic management in NPOs to attain the research objectives.

The focus of the study was to discover an area of investigation archetypal of the major features of NPOs and an analytic open to strategic management. Firstly, ten NPOs were selected, which embody five attributes namely; -

- Organised and possess certain institutional realities- such as having an organised system of governance, policies, strategic plans, workplace policies and defined organisations behaviours

- Are private and tend to be institutionally distinct from government;
- Are non-profit-distributing and do not return any profit they make to donors or owners
- Are intrinsically voluntary and participating is not compulsory;
- Have reported steady growth in the last decade.

Being a phenomenological Study, data collected by interviews help identify and interpret a participant's perceptions and constructed meanings. Document analysis was also used to compare the meanings to already documented ones (Creswell 1998). The significance of selecting a phenomenological study was to facilitate the pursuit of knowledge and personal construction of meanings.

3.4 Research Method

In line with the objectives of this research, exploratory research was the selected strategy as it is proven to explain how and why something should happen efficiently. The study used exploratory research owing to the qualitative nature of the research questions and objectives, which are oriented towards determining meanings associated with strategic management practices in NPOs in the UK. According to Wilson and Chaddha (2010), exploratory research is useful for identifying and resolving interplay of research participants' perspectives regarding a research phenomenon within a social or organisational setting. Collection of data was through secondary research and primary research.

3.4.1 Secondary Research

Secondary research is a common research technique, making use of already published reported data (usually for a different reason) to the focus of the current study. An advantage of this research method is that the data is readily available. An obstacle in this method was the lack of specificity, and this was highlighted by the limited data available on the use of strategy tools in NPO's in the UK, the strategy process/stages of NPO's in the UK, and NPO competition in the UK. For this study, secondary documentary data was applied to contextualise primary data. In line with secondary research, document analysis was used.

3.4.2 Primary Research

After a review of the secondary sources of data, the next step entailed collecting primary data. Primary data is a research type that involves the self-collection of data, in this case, it was by the use of semi-structured face to face interviews, to be held in the interviewees own environment. This was to enable the interviewee to be at ease in their familiar business environment when discussing the topic. It was also to take into consideration that all interviewees were volunteers whose time is valuable and may assist in the decision-making process of the individual's availability to volunteer.

3.4.3 Semi-structured Interview

The study used semi-structured interviews: as qualitative research instruments, semi-structured interviews facilitate a study of individuals' perspectives, perceptions, opinions, viewpoints, meanings, and expectations. They facilitate an understanding of entrenched perceptions, and at the same time call upon comprehensible images or pictures of a research situation (Onwuegbuzie *et al.* 2012). The study used semi-structured interviews to complement document analysis, in the expectation that they would offer a deepened account of the attitudes, practices, and behaviours of leaders who use strategic management approaches in NPOs.

Use of semi-structured interviews allowed the participants to expand on issues they felt noteworthy for the study. It also:

- Allowed the researcher to ask questions outside the scope of review to facilitate research.
- Facilitated probing and asking follow-up questions.
- Can stimulate an emergence of unexpected concepts yet also facilitated the use of 'vignette questions.'

Overall, the interviews range from being conversational to occasionally being rigid.

3.4.4 Other interview methods considered

Interviews were not done via questionnaire as it removes the ability to reiterate or reword questions if they do not address the original question. This could be said for surveys, which are a rigid form of questioning and may only provide a limited amount of data

3.4.5 Document Analysis

The study also used document analysis, as the process of document analysis was expected to balance data collected through interviews. As Onwuegbuzie *et al.* (2012) pointed out, document analysis can be used in combination with methods of research to add-on data collected and realise triangulation. The process of using document analysis involved a systematic review, evaluation, and interpretation of varied documents to deduce meanings and develop a profound understanding of how NPOs in the UK approach and use strategic management models. Document analysis was appropriate for the study, since it enabled access to information that was initially difficult to access in circumstances where participants were inaccessible. The method also eliminated 'research effect' to maintain a high level of objectivity in the data analysis process. 'Research effect' refers to cases whereby a researcher integrates personal assumptions during the process of data analysis to influence the research results. The underlying motivation for using document analysis was due to the expectation of enabling a higher level of scrutiny of changing trends of strategic management approaches in the NPOs in the UK. Research reports, sectoral reports, and institutional reports enabled the researcher to track changes in strategic management practices over time.

3.5 Sampling Procedures

Before active collection of data, the researchers selected a sample of participants using a non-probability sampling method called convenience sampling. It was considered appropriate for the study as it potentially facilitates the selection of participants based on how accessible they are and their willingness to take part in the study. The process of sampling entailed selection of a small sample of managers or leaders of NPOs in the UK to represent the population of study. Using convenience sampling method, the researcher managed to access seven participants from seven NPOs in the UK – although the researcher had targeted 15 participants from 10 NPOs. Therefore, participants were selected depending on their knowledge of strategic management in their organisations, in addition to their willingness to take part in the study. The participants selected to take part in the study jointly exemplified the perspectives of the management and leadership of NPOs in the UK.

The convenience sampling criterion was appropriate, but had drawbacks, owing to its nature of being non-random. The researcher understood that there was a possibility that the sample selected would not necessarily represent the entire population of NPOs managers the study focused on. For this reason, the research approach is a comparatively weak sampling method. As a result, the research had minimal control over the sample's representativeness. Hence, the sample selected had a potential bias.

After sample selection, semi-structured interviews were undertaken in the seven NPOs targeted. The semi-structured interviews were undertaken with leaders of the organisations, mainly project managers, senior officers, coordinators, and CEOs. Basing on the interview questions on the literature, all interviews took an average of 50 minutes.

3.5.1 Potential risks and challenges

When conducting these interviews various situations could occur

Table 3.5.1 Situation, impact and preventative measures		
Situation	Impact	Preventative
Traffic/transport problems	Late or not able to attend	Keep the contact details of the interviewee to hand to communicate in any eventuality
Recording issues	Poor quality recording or fail to record	Produce a test recording in each environment first. Followed by a double check that the equipment is recording before starting the interviews
Withdrawal of consent	No interview	Find alternative if pool is too small
Sickness from either party	Delayed or no other date available	Keep the contact details of the interviewee to hand to communicate in any eventuality and send confirmation and share contact details.

3.6 Data analysis

Analysis of data collected was performed using thematic analysis, which requires the use of four key steps for extraction of meaning. It was based on Miles and Huberman's (1994) framework for data analysis to facilitate extractions of meanings through:

- data reduction,
- data display,
- drawing conclusion
- verification of findings.

These translate to different phases like familiarisation with data, generation of initial codes, extracting themes, review of themes, definition, and naming of themes and generation of the report.

Table 3.1. Phases of thematic analysis [Adapted from McLeod (2017)]

	PHASES	DESCRIPTION OF ANALYSIS PROCESS
1	Familiarising myself with data	i) Narrative preparation, i.e. transcribing data ii) (Re-)reading the data and noting down initial ideas
2	Generating initial codes	i) Coding interesting features of the data in a systematic fashion across entire data set ii) Collating data relevant to each code
3	Searching for themes	i) Collating codes into potential themes ii) Gathering all data relevant to each potential theme
4	Reviewing themes	i) Checking if themes work in relation to the coded extracts ii) Checking if themes work in relation to the entire data set iii) Reviewing data to search for additional themes iv) Generating a thematic "map" of the analysis
5	Defining and naming themes	i) On-going analysis to refine the specifics of each theme and the overall story the analysis tells ii) Generating clear definitions and names for each theme
6	Producing the report	i) Selection of vivid, compelling extract examples ii) Final analysis of selected extracts iii) Relating the analysis back to the research question, objectives and previous literature reviewed

Data collected was initially passed through a process of data reduction, to identify key categories that were viewed to potentially address the research objectives, and at this stage, redundant data was discarded. The next stage included the data display process (Guest et al., 2011). It helped organise and assemble data to ensure they are compact and straightforward. Afterward, conclusions were drawn to assist in the selection of relevant data patterns or themes in line with the research questions (Flick, 2014; Mason, 2002). The last stage involved data verification process (Thomas and Harden 2008; Bryman, 2008). Personal connections through the researcher's network of acquaintances were instrumental in recruiting the participants. The participants were first contacted by a covering email to get their permission to conduct an interview. In two of the cases where the employees were interviewed, their HR department was contacted through a covering mail that explained the nature of the study.

In the process of data analysis, the identified data categories were then passed through a process of data display to organise and bring together data, to make them easily accessible, clear-cut, and compressed to facilitate easy generation of meaning. The next process involved the process of drawing conclusion, which entailed selection of relevant themes. Afterward, the process of data verification followed, this involved pragmatic review and assessment of the conclusions to determine their accuracy.

Figure 3.1. Conceptual diagram of a data analysis

Figure 3.1. Conceptual diagram of a data analysis

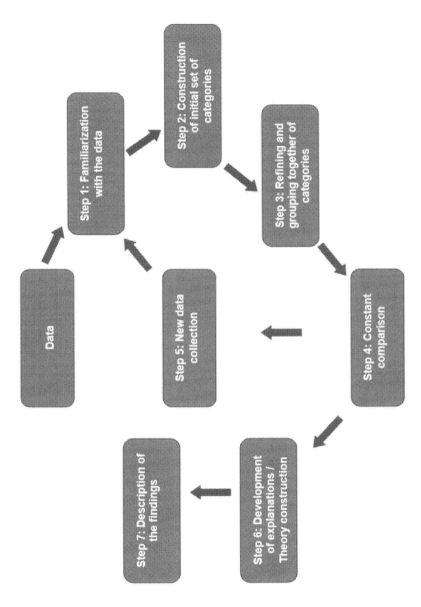

3.7 Ethical Considerations

Participants were issued with a consent form and information sheet (See Appendix 1 and 2), that clarified to them the reasons for undertaking the study, what may be required from them in the process of the research, the benefits of taking part in the study, why they are an integral part of this research, the benefits and risks they may be exposed to by taking part in the study, and their primary rights as participants.

All of those interviewed requested that their identities and organisations remain anonymous, the researcher treated their anonymity as an elemental ethical precondition. Although the number of research participants was comparatively small, their perspectives covered a broad scope of stakeholder perceptions, in addition to the totality of their perceptions about strategic management in NPOs in the U.K.

To ensure that they also understood the content of the information sheet, the researcher explained to the research participants the study objectives, the methods to be used, the demands the research places on the participants, and the risks that they may face as research participants. The process was expected to make sure that participants were not coerced into taking part in the study. It was also expected to ensure that the research participants adequately understand the right information or the implications of their involvement before willingly agreeing to take part in the study. The participants were also informed that they have a right to withdraw from the study at any point during the interview.

To guarantee the confidentiality of collected data, the researcher maintained personal control and access to the data collected: data was stored on a password-protected computer, participants' identities were kept anonymous, and other identifying information was not disclosed (including specific names of their organisations) to ensure maximum anonymity. Some participants raised concerns regarding a need for total obscurity as the number of donors they can appeal to is contingent on the quality of reputation they command. Also, the answers provided were used exclusively for the study. No third party has access or physically handle the recording or the transcripts.

3.8 Research limitations

As previously mentioned, lack of prior research studies in this field has limited the scope of the research via secondary data.

Sample size - fortunately, it was not difficult to find relationships in the data. The not for profit sector in the UK is vast, and ideally a larger sample size of interviewees would help obtain a realistic representative of the industry and the risk of the data having little relationships was quite high.

Bias - either conscience or not, biases are where the interviewee represents their organisation or themselves in an inaccurate way. This bias could reflect the reliance of the data for the research, and if any detection of bias in research is thought- it will be highlighted in the relevant section that the answer relates to. This is to avoid perpetuating that bias on the rest of the data.

4.0 Research Findings

This chapter presents analyses of data collected and is based on data-driven themes, which are based on the research questions that guided the study. Seven participants from seven NPOs were accessed and their responses were analysed concurrently before being compared against each other. This chapter presents analysis and interpretation of data collected by relating them to the findings of several literature streams outlined in Chapter 2: Literature Review.

Several themes are described regarding the accompanying research findings and the results obtained form the foundation for the conclusion in the final chapter. The analysis of research data was carried out basing on the participants' words before being interpreted into results by integrating them with relevant literature. To guarantee anonymity, the participants and organisations are not referred to using their names. Instead, they are tagged as P1 at NGO1 for the first participant and first organisation or P2 and NGO2 for the second participant and second organisation.

Participant mix

- P1 has 12 years of experience as a human resource manager at NPO1, which is a humanitarian NGO.
- P2 is a program development manager with seven years of experience at NPO2, which is a development NGO.

- P3 is a CEO with 5 years of experience at a charity that specialises in child care.
- P4 is a project manager with 2 years experiences at a NPO4, a religious organisation.
- P5 is a program coordinator at an NPO4, which is a community foundation,
- P6 is a human resource manager at NPO 5, a social advocacy organisation,
- P7 is a project manager at NPO6, a charity supporting a social economic disadvantage community.
- P8 has 7 years' experience as the chair of the board for a national children's charity (withdrawn).
- P9 is a CEO of a national charity based in London with 6 years experiences (withdrawn).
- P10 has 20 years' experience working for a regional charity supporting disabled adults (withdrawn).

Consistent with the research questions, questions asked that guided the research

- What are the Strategic Management Practices that your organisation uses?

- What are the Strategic Models that your organisation uses?

- In what ways do your Strategic Management Practices differ from those of for-profit organisations?

- Looking at how your organisation's strategies can you tell me how they have been influenced by:

a) The external environmental

b) The internal context

c) Strategy formation processes

- In response to the above, how does your organisation set up strategic management strategies in response to changes in:

    a) The internal environment?

    b) The external environment?

- Please tell me what reasons underlie the use of strategic management in your organisation?

What are the Strategic Management Practices that your organisation uses?

P1, P2, P5, and P7 believed their strategic management practices are largely influenced by external factors like donors and clients, who have dominant control over who should control the capital, legitimacy, and labour. As they have scarce resources, donors have greater leverage over the practices they should adopt to appeal to them.

P1 said: "Our organisation's strategic management practice mainly entails sitting down whenever there is a foreseeable problem in our future external problem to put up goals and a vision that is capable of provides a sense of purpose and direction for each one in the organisation and those we related with, like our donors."

P2 said: Consistent with these assumptions, Rehor et al. (2014) argued that a significant number of dynamics of shifts to the external environment and the complexity of the entire strategic management process. They also showed that the failure or success of NPOs is essentially contingent on strategic decision-making. This indicates that strategic management practices are largely influenced by external stakeholders and designed for problem-solving. According to Rehor et al. (2014), they are a combination of management decisions and action plans that the management can employ to enable competitive advantage and long-term better performance of an organisation. Therefore, it potentially reduces organisational weaknesses and leverages their strengths by anticipating prospects and problems.

P3 had their strategic management practices oriented towards the internal environment.

P3 said: "We do a lot in terms of strategic management... As the CEO, I have done much to develop an organisational culture that enables each member of the organisation to identify and develop a sense of belonging and shared values to attain future goals.... By members of the organisation, I mean the board, management, and general staff. Our strategic management has been instrumental in enhancing each member's level of motivation to attain common goals.

It is only P4 and P6, whose strategic management practices are aimed at both the internal and external environment.

P4 said: "I have been greatly involved in setting up strategic management practice, which in my opinion are tactical managerial decisions and skills that directly affect our organisation's capacity to respond to the needs of our beneficiaries and wishes of our funders and the needs of our employees. We set up strategic plans and goals with a focus on those areas, and to ultimately move in a new direction whenever there is a problem.

P4 and P6 attempted to show that what is significant for strategic management practices is making sure that focus is placed on both external and internal strategic objectives. Their body language was very open and confident for both participants and this enabled the researcher to believe their accounts as accurate.

Related literature has indicated that strategic management should make sure that organisational management does not occur randomly but that they are based on clarified long-term objectives (Weerawardena & Mort, 2012). Weerawardena and Mort (2012) also clarified that NPO leaders should be open to shifting goals and activities with regards to changing situations in the external or internal environments. As a result, organisational leaders need to consistently, monitor, evaluate, and benefit from constant feedback. It is on this basis that strategic management could be reasoned as a fluid, and ongoing approach, as opposed to a one-shot approach. Rehor et al. (2014) also argued that strategic management should also be considered as a process and a means of contemplating about particular aspects of an organisation, like long- and short-term goals, stakeholders, and achieving efficiency. It is a continuous intricate process of management that agrees on the organisational targets and a strategic course for reaching specific targets.

To this end, it can only be concluded that a majority of the NPOs in the UK have defective strategic management practices targeted at external environment, other than both the internal and external environment.

P2 said that their organisation is overwhelmed by the growing number of NPOs that compete for funds, which forces them to focus their strategies on winning the increasingly scarce donors. That they must ensure that the organisation is sustainable in the long term. Consistent with this, Mort and Weerawardena (2008) established that more NPOs are focusing on ensuring the sustainability. However, they appear to disagree with P2. They assert that non-profit literature seems not to reveal that NPOs have emphasised on attaining competitive advantages to enable them to grow and survive over the long-term, despite an increasing rate of threats to their sustainability. Weerawardena et al. (2010) had also observed that NPOs must lay a comparatively lower emphasis on clients than on donors.

What are the Strategic Models that your organisation uses?

All participants showed that their organisations are niche strategists, which Ogonji (2014) defines as "organisations that stick to their missions and objectives and have not considered had expanded beyond their niche." Only NGO4 has attempted to use a market-orientation model to get money flowing into NGO4, which is an educational foundation.

P4 said: "We are an educational foundation. Providing bursaries to students in and outside the UK is becoming very much costly. On the other hand, we have had few donations coming in the last couple of years. However, we learned that the more students we sponsor, the more attractive our organisation looks. So, we want as much as possible to treat our clients well. When they speak well of us, more money keeps on coming.

The focus of NGO4 is appealing and satisfying customers, consistent with this, Weerawardena et al. (2010) demonstrated that few NPOs use the "market orientation" model and the "market-driven firm paradigm," which are substantially employed in for-profit organisations to satisfy and retain customers. However, there seems to be discontent with NGO4's approach in current literature. Weerawardena et al. (2010) argued that while focusing on clients has a potential to ensure better service delivery in NPOs, the link between the clients and generation of revenue is fundamentally detached in NPOs.

P1, P2, P3, P6, and P7 use the donor-oriented model to appeal to more funding from donors.

P2 said: "I don't believe what we do is unique. As there is an implied understanding that the type of sector we operate in has an unwritten rule that we are not allowed to engage in active marketing, the way we can advertise ourselves to donors is limited, unless of course there is a humanitarian crisis. So, we want to be as transparent as possible, to be as accountable as possible and to rely on word-of-mouth advertising to tell our able donors that their funds are helping a social cause."

From the review of the literature, there is a considerable understanding that NPOs use donor-oriented models of strategic management (Weerawardena et al. 2010). They place donors at the centre of their appeal, owing to the decisive role they play in the provision of revenue stream that is significant for the operation of an NPO.

The approach pursued by a majority of NPOs in the UK, whereby they emphasise donor-oriented models is inconsistent with Weerawardena's et al. (2010) idea that NPOs could focus on 'balancing money and mission' as the principal concern in the management of NPOs. Weerawardena's et al. (2010) considered organisations that use this model as characterised by using constructs like production quality, pricing, production quantity, improvement of service quality, and budgeting practice.

Evidently, a majority of NPOs in the UK have not considered using the 'earned income strategies' and "market-oriented model." In the last decade, some scholars have arrived at a consensus that 'earned income strategies' can be used to attain organisational sustainability, which integrates the attributes of non-profit with for-profit organisations (Peredo & McLean, 2006; Weerawardena et al. (2010). The profits that these organisations generate from their principal activities are applied in engaging in numerous social ventures (Seelos & Mair, 2005).

In what ways do your Strategic Management Practices differ from those of for-profit organisations?

All seven participants agreed that external environmental and internal environment influences the strategy formation processes and the strategies use. This is despite the idea that four of the participants have strategic management practices principally designed for the external environment.

P2 said: "Both the external and internal environment threatens our existence. But, I have worked here long enough as a human resource manager to understand that the organisation is more terrified by the idea of increasingly diminishing donations and funding from the government than the relatively high employee turnover."

P5 said that their organisation had realised a need to develop new missions annually to appeal to a new base of donors, who may favour a newer mission. These ideas were explored in previous research, and according to Othman et al. (2014), because of slow funding, non-profit managers increasingly realise that their new missions are to constantly, influence donors to donate, volunteers to volunteer, clients to come for help, and employees to be client-friendly, accountable and transparent. Some scholars have argued that adopting resource-based strategies can enable NPOs to adopt a change of attitude with respect to obtaining and managing their funding sources and their management strategies. Put differently, NPOs must seek ways to efficiently manage their resources more efficiently to improve their performance in an increasingly complex internal and external environment (Macedo & Pinho 2004; Othman et al. 2014).

While P3 agreed that their organisation must monitor the internal and external environment constantly, they also have to constantly protect their key resources, including the board, which is made up of funders and managers, and the need for them to constantly plan for the future. An earlier study demonstrated that some of the internal indicators that enhance the urgency for planning, particularly in the increasingly aggressive non-profit environment. These include periods of stagnant organisational growth and administrative operations, and high employee turnover or changes in leadership (Giffords and Dina 2004). P3's assumption is built on the resource dependence theory, which contends that organisations can attain ultimate survival depending on their capacity to obtain and maintain resources (Pfeffer and Salancik, 1978, p. 2).

However, the tendency to focus on the internal environment by NPOs in the UK is not advocated in current literature. According to Giffords and Dina (2004), a tendency to concentrate on the internal environment would enable the managers to discover conflicting perspectives of the organisation's mission and vision, and degree of efficiency. However, they may as well find themselves becoming increasingly immersed in the everyday operation of the organisations, which, in turn, may influence them to concentrate on the "program ends rather than the purpose" such as attending to the needs of the service users. Hence, while organisational cultures and values should be taken into consideration, as they directly affect the organisation's operation, external factors like client needs and donor demands should also be considered (Romney, 2001). This is because the external environment is also crucial for effective functioning of NPOs, particularly in periods where there is a high competition for limited funds, changes in client priorities, Shifts in accreditation requirements, and societal changes (Romney, 2001).

P4 and P6 stated that their organisations have always aimed to achieve a balance between addressing their external and internal environmental problems, as part of their long-term strategy. According to Giffords and Dina (2004), the main advantage of creating a strategic plan within the framework of CQPI is to enable non-profit's management and employees to acclimatise the organisation to the existing internal and external environment, prioritise the organisation's mission, and illuminate client's needs. This will enable NPOs to continually improve quality services to their clients while revealing to their funders and other concerned stakeholders that the organisation has a positive effect on them.

Looking at how your organisation's strategies can you tell me how they have been influenced by:

1) The internal environmental
2) The external factors
3) Strategy formation processes

All the seven participants agreed that external environmental and internal environment influences the strategy formation processes and the strategies use, they had differing responses to how they respond to the internal and external environment.

Internal Environment

Regarding the internal context, P1, P2, P3, and P4 expressed that their organisation' strategic plans are affected by the internal environment.

P1 said: "Since the managers are the ones who have to implement the strategic plans, the failure or success of the plans depends mostly on them. The successful plans we have had in the last six months have succeeded because of the experienced managers we have. It's fair to say that our plans to have a successful strategy logistics during disasters is due to the experiences we have acquired through previous projects."

This indicates that the success of strategic plans chiefly depends on the experiences of the management along with the accumulated knowledge accumulated over time.

P2 said: "For a strategic plan to be successful, a manager has to have skills on how to work in a team, and create fits between the strategic plan and how the organisation operates.

From P2's statement, it is apparent that for a strategic plan to be both effective and successful, the manager who develops and carries out the strategy must have essential management skills, like building strong organisational cultures that can be instrumental in implementing the strategy, as well as have organisational skills. Evidently, an organisation's context influences how to implement the strategic plans.

P3 had their strategic management practices oriented towards the internal environment. P3 said: "We do a lot in terms of strategic management… I have developed an organisational culture that enables everyone to identify and develop a sense of belonging and shared values to attain future goals…. Our strategic management has been instrumental in enhancing each member's level of motivation to attain common goals."

P4 said: "Our strategic plans have generally been successful, the organisational resources, and *sometimes* the structure, have played a role in making sure that we attract large donations from other external organisations. A good information system and finance systems to advertise ourselves enhance how we communicate with the donors. In the case of structure, when you have better pay packages that motivate your staff, they become motivated to implement any plan without any question of resistance."

From P4's statement, organisation resources and structure play a crucial role in influencing how effectively a strategic plan can be implemented. At the same time, an effective reward system plays a crucial role in influencing the implementation of a strategic plan, as it influences employee and managers' level of performance in terms of implementing the plan. Organisation resources and structure play a crucial role in influencing the outcome of a strategic plan and in this regard, when an organisation's resources are not used to the advantage of an organisation, it is possible that the resources are likely to become a waste, which encumbers effective development and implementation of a strategic plan. The issue of organisational structure is, therefore, important and demonstrates how an organisation's policies can either hasten or decelerate the implementation process by either motivating or de-motivating the staff.

The issue of resources also appears to be treated seriously by P4's organisation. It shows that when an NPO has good resources, such as information systems and finances, it is likely to have an effective strategic plan. In this regard, information systems have a potential to influence how efficiently an NPO carries out its communication plan while developing and implementing a strategy. Similarly, finances also determine the effectiveness of strategic plans, including by affecting how other resources, like labor or advertising, can be procured to implement a plan.

The issue of organisational culture is critical, and effect how people behave and respond to the plan. In other words, supportive cultures like collective identities and acceptable behaviors contribute to a low potential for employees to resist a plan. When a manager builds strong cultures that identify with a plan, he is likely to face a minimal level of resistance. In the process of assessing the internal environment of an NPO, it is possible for the management to identify an organisation's contradictory perspectives, such as the mission and the level of efficiency. The issue of organisational missions and values are viewed as important as members of staff who work in an NPO, as they are likely to find themselves engrossed in their organisation's day by day operations.

According to Othman *et al.* (2014), because of slow funding, non-profit managers increasingly realise that their new missions are to influence donors to donate, volunteers to volunteer, clients to come for help, and employees to be client-friendly, accountable and transparent. Some scholars have argued that adopting resource-based strategies can enable NPOs to adopt a change of attitude with respect to obtaining and managing their funding sources and their management strategies. Put differently, NPOs must seek ways to efficiently manage their resources efficiently to improve their performance in an increasingly a complex internal environment (Macedo and Pinho 2004; Othman *et al.* 2014).

Giffords and Dina (2004) observe that while evaluating an NPO's internal environment, the managers may discover conflicting perspectives of the organisation's mission and vision, and degree of efficiency. Giffords and Dina (2004) expressed concern that individuals working in NPOs may find themselves becoming immersed in the everyday operation of the organisations, which may influence them to concentrate on "program ends rather than the purpose". Organisational cultures and values should as well be taken into consideration as they directly affect the organisation's operation (Giffords and Dina, 2004). When the leadership of the organisation seeks to create a strategic plan, they need first to undertake an internal analysis to discover issues that potentially affect the organisation. Afterward, they should position those deemed vital within their organisation's context.

While P3 agreed that their organisation must monitor the internal environment, they must protect their key resources, including the board, which is made up of the funders, the managers, and the need for future planning. These include periods of stagnant organisational growth and administrative operations, and high employee turnover or changes in leadership (Giffords and Dina 2004). P3's assumption is built on the resource dependence theory, which contends that organisations can attain ultimate survival depending on their capacity to obtain and maintain resources (Pfeffer and Salancik, 1978, p. 2).

The tendency to focus on the internal environment by NPOs in the UK is not advocated in current literature. According to Giffords and Dina (2004), a tendency to concentrate on the internal environment would enable the managers may discover conflicting perspectives of the organisation's mission and vision, and degree of efficiency. They may find themselves becoming increasingly immersed in the everyday operation of the organisations, which, in turn, may influence them to concentrate on the "program ends rather than the purpose" that they are intended to accomplish, including attending to the needs of the clients. Hence, while organisational cultures and values should as well be taken into consideration, as they directly affect the organisation's operation, external factors like client needs and donor demands should also be considered (Romney, 2001). The external environment is also crucial for the well-functioning of NPOs, particularly in periods where there is a high competition for limited funds, changes in client priorities, shifts in accreditation requirements, and societal changes (Romney, 2001).

P4 and P6 stated that their organisations have always aimed to achieve a balance between addressing their external and internal environmental problems, as part of their long-term strategy. According to Giffords and Dina (2004), the main advantage of creating a strategic plan, within the framework of CQPI, is to enable nonprofit's management and employees to acclimatise the organisation to the existing internal and external environment, priorities the organisation's mission, and illuminate client's needs. This will enable NPOs to continually improve quality services to their clients while revealing to their funders and other concerned stakeholders that the organisation has a positive effect on them.

External factors

Some of the participants also mentioned that they have strategic management practices principally designed to respond to the external environment.

P1, P2, P5, and P7 believed their strategic management practices are influenced by external factors like donors and clients, who have dominant control over who should control the capital, legitimacy, and labor. As they have scarce resources, donors have greater leverage over the practices they should adopt to appeal to them.

P1 said: "Our organisation's strategic management practice is whenever there is a foreseeable external problem, to put up goals and a vision that is capable of providing a sense of purpose and direction for everyone in the organisation and those we related with, like our donors."

P2 said: "Both the external and internal environment threatens our existence… I have worked here long enough to understand that the organisation is more terrified by the idea of increasingly diminishing donations and funding from the government than the high employee turnover."

P5 said that their organisation had realised a need to develop new missions annually to appeal to a new base of donors who may favor a newer mission. It is only P4 and P6, whose strategic management practices are aimed at external environment.

P4 said: "I have been involved in setting up strategic management practice, which in my opinion are tactical managerial decisions and skills that affect our organisation's capacity to respond to the needs of our beneficiaries, wishes of our funders, and the needs of our employees. We set up strategic plans and goals with a focus on those areas, and to ultimately move in a new direction whenever there is a problem.

P4 and P6 attempted to show that what is significant for strategic management practices is making sure that focus is placed on both external and internal strategic objectives.

Consistent with these assumptions, Rehor *et al.* (2014) argued that a number of dynamics of shifts to the external environment and the complexity of the entire strategic management process. They also showed that the failure or success of NPOs is contingent on strategic decision-making. This indicates that strategic management practices are influenced by external stakeholders and designed for problem-solving. According to Rehor *et al.* (2014), they are a combination of management decisions and action plans that the management can employ to enable competitive advantage and long-term better performance of an organisation.

Consequently, it potentially reduces organisational weaknesses and leverages their strengths by anticipating prospects and problems.

Related literature has indicated that strategic management should make sure that organisational management does not occur randomly, but that they are based on clarified long-term objectives on how to respond to the external environment (Weerawardena and Mort, 2012). Weerawardena and Mort (2012) also clarified that NPO leaders should be open to shifting goals and activities with regards to changing situations in the external environment. As a result, organisational leaders need to consistently monitor, evaluate, and benefit from constant feedback. It is on this basis that strategic management could be viewed as a fluid, and ongoing approach, as opposed to a one-shot approach. Rehor *et al.* (2014) also argued that strategic management should also be considered as a process and a means of contemplating about particular aspects of an organisation, like long- and short-term goals, stakeholders, and achieving efficiency. It is a continuous intricate process of management that agrees on the organisational targets and a strategic course for reaching specific targets.

P2 said that the growing number of NPOs that compete for funds forces them to focus their strategies on winning the increasingly scarce donors overwhelms their organisation. Consistent with this, Mort and Weerawardena (2008) established that NPOs are focusing on ensuring the sustainability. They appear to disagree with P2 when they assert that nonprofit literature seems not to reveal that NPOs have emphasized on attaining competitive advantages to enable them to grow and survive over the long-term, despite an increasing rate of threats to their sustainability.

Weerawardena *et al.* (2010) had also observed that NPOs must lay a comparatively lower emphasis on clients than on donors.

To this end, it can only be concluded that a majority of the NPOs in the UK have defective strategic management practices targeted at external environment, other than both the internal and external environment.

Strategy formation process

P3 and P6 suggested that that the strategy formation process plays a role in determining the goals and mission of a strategic plan.

P3 said: "One important aspect is its capacity to direct the goals of strategies that we develop. When developing our strategic plan, we usually find it easy explaining to others the mission of our strategic plans."

P6 said that a strategy formation process is indispensable in NPOs today as it permits managers first to do a thorough assessment of their external and internal environments, which offers information that guides strategic planning. From the statement, it becomes apparent that a central element of a strategy statement is to develop the key objectives, and that it, in turn, serves as a medium for attaining goals of a strategic plan.

Related to this perspective, Analoui and Samour (2012) argued that strategy formulation process enables NPOs to focus their activities for strategic planning on the mission and measures of performance, as well as in creating mission, vision, and value that should guide strategic planning. In Weerasooriya's *et al.* (2014) view, a vital attribute of strategic formulation process is that managers assess the external and internal environment to assist in setting goals of a strategic plan. It becomes clear that strategy formation process should be a process of selecting the most suitable course of action that can help attain organisational goals and objectives, and in the process, achieve the organisational mission. Towards this end, a strategic formation process is a crucial phase in the strategic management process that assists NPOs to formulate and develop strategies targeted at attaining the goals of strategic planning based on the results found from an assessment of the organisation's environment.

In response to the above, how does your organisation set up strategic management strategies in response to changes in:

    a.   The external environment?

    b.   The internal environment?

All participants mentioned that they rely on strategic planning to set up strategic management strategies.

The external environment

P3 considers strategic planning as an ongoing process for supporting the NPOs to achieve a continually improving quality service to their beneficiaries or target population, while at the same time showing the donors, funders, and community some positive effects of their services on those they serve.

P6 also showed that they respond to the changing needs of the donors or funders through capacity building. To successfully respond to the external environment, their organisation carries out capacity building as a continual event instead of a one-time event, including by building effective teams and creating frameworks that can ensure effective performance to ensure a lasting appeal to donors.

P4 said: "We have traditionally used strategic planning but it's a complex problem-solving process for the future. I guess that's how it should be described." P7 said that they first evaluate an organisation's performance and identify areas where there is a need to execute targeted improvements rapidly.

There is an agreement in current research regarding the use of frameworks that can help them to set up strategic management strategies. The participants did not mention any of strategic planning processes by name, however, they appeared to focus on the continuous process of evaluating their external environments. This form of the strategic planning process is what Giffords and Dina (2004) call CQPI. As Giffords and Dina (2004) elaborated, most NPOs use CQPI to adjust to the changing external and internal environments. Pecora and Seelig (2001), who consider a CQPI plan as a systematic process that enables NPOs to set up plans to improve in all areas of their operation, support the idea. Giffords and Dina (2004) view it as an organisation's pledge to its clients and the greater community to offer them efficient and effective services. According to Mikulas and Cohan (2001), setting up a CQPI means that that the planning, goal-setting and attainment activities of an organisation are provided with information using a formal feedback process, including through external assessments, to bring about improved performance that is beneficial to both the organisation and its constituents.

The Internal Environment

The participants' organisations sets up strategic management strategies in response to internal changes differently. Only P3 explained how their organisations respond to changes in the internal environment.

P3 said that their organisations tended to delay strategic planning, yet explained that this because of very compelling reasons, such as cash flow challenges or inability to access the human resource to undertake a strategic plan. Analoui and Samour (2012) explained that deliberately delaying strategic planning is a form of strategic management that is particularly necessary in cases where an organisation undergoes a cash flow crisis, and as a result, needs to access greater finances first before responding to a crisis. This is common with NPOs that lack sufficient funds to implement their strategies and may be a risk management technique an organisation uses from experiencing financial challenges.

Regarding P3's idea that an organisation may delay strategic planning because of an inability to access the suitable human resource to undertake a strategic plan, there appears to be an agreement in the literature that some NPOs find it convenient delaying strategic planning because of problems with personnel. As Analoui and Samour (2012) explained, a convincing reason why this may happen is if an organisation faces a leadership crisis, particularly when a key leadership position must be filled to spearhead the strategies planned. According to Analoui and Samour

(2012), this strategic management practice usually happens when an NPO is in a transition period and as a result seeks an executive director position who can effectively engage in a strategic planning process.

P3 further elaborated on how their organisation tends to postpone strategic planning particularly in situations where proper skills, commitment, and resources are lacking that can generate and implement a solid plan. Analoui and Samour (2012) agree with such measures of strategic management. They opined that lack of a skilled workforce to carry out a plan could make strategic planning in NPOs to be a waste of time. When such elements are lacking to involve all internal stakeholders than an NPO can put itself in a far worse financial and reputational problem. Hence, a lacking internal capacity may serve as an internal problem, that NPOs respond to by postponing strategic planning until they restructure themselves. From P3's statement, strategic planning should not be pursued by an NPO when its effective implementation is highly improbable.

Please tell me what reasons underlie the use of strategic management in your organisation?

The participants suggested varied reasons that motivate their organisations to engage in strategic management. P1, P2, P5, and P7 mentioned that they engage in strategic planning to overcome the competition for donations. All participants mentioned that they resort to strategic planning when they face problems in the acquisition of finances. P3 and P4 mentioned that they considered engaging strategic management when looking for partnerships with other organisations. P4 and P6 stated that they considered it appropriate to engage in strategic management to respond to a need for transparency and accountability by their donors. All the participants agree that strategic planning enabled them to make informed decisions regarding their futures.

These views are adequately supported in the previous literature. According to Ogonji (2014), strategic management enables organisations to adjust to environmental factors that may threaten their futures, and to agree on what should be done to get there by adopting new approaches. Bryson (2010) established that strategic management encourages strategic thinking and actions to respond to a situational issue in an organisation. It leads to a clarification of vision, assists organisations to discover best strategies, promotes consensus building among stakeholders and improves the capacity of organisations to make a quality decision that reflects organisational objectives and mission.

The researcher also outlined that strategic management also becomes useful when organisations change their scope of operation or mission. Bryson (2010) and Ogonji (2014) agreed that it is the challenges that NPOs must address in the internal and external environments that motivate them to set up strategic management measures. The researchers outlined that rise in demand for services that NPOs offer : a greater level of competition : problems in the acquisition of funds : a desire to collaborate with other organisations : greater pressures for transparency and accountability : increased levels of doubt regarding economic : and political and social changes of the future, prompted NPOs to engage in strategic management.

The participants show a need for NPOs to think strategically, in addition to the belief that carrying out strategic management brings about positive outcomes on the performance of organisations. The participant's NPOs are attempting to run their organisations as business enterprises to contend with the competition for funding, investing in enhancing their professional competences using strategic planning.

There comes a question regarding the need to locate suitable methods that can permit NPOs to resolve some fundamental issues regarding their purposes, such as what they are attempting to attain, in addition to how they establish and attain their goals and missions. As can be discerned from the P4 and P6's response, that their organisations consider engaging in strategic management to respond to a need for transparency and accountability by their donors. It becomes clear that strategic planning has become indispensable for modern NPOs that want to make informed decisions regarding their future. Such a fundamental question falls into the dominion of the idea of strategic management.

5.0 Results and Discussion

This section presents and discusses the results of the findings established through the analysis, before being interpreted through perspectives of several literature streams that are outlined in Chapter 4 are presented. The results are described proportionate to their associated research findings.

Result 1: Strategic management practices used by NPOs in the UK

A majority of the participants elaborated that strategic management practices are influenced by external factors like donors and clients, who have dominant control over who should control the capital, legitimacy, and labor. As NPOs have scarce financial resources and depend on their donors, the donors have greater leverage over the practices they should adopt to appeal to them. This reasoning has a theoretical basis, as it is well explained by the resource dependence theory, which hypothesizes that an organisation's behavior depends on the degree of its resource dependencies (Hillman *et al*. 2009). In other words, external factors like donors are always bound to influence the strategies and decisions of NPOs.

NPOs make strategic management practices to survive, yet since they require resources like capital, labor, legitimacy, and clientele, their strategy depends on the external factors control, which causes interdependencies that may contribute to an imbalance of power over who should control the NPOs. Since the finances they require in their operations are scarce, the funders or donors have greater power. This potentially leads the organisation to lose autonomy and an ability to freely undertake managerial and strategic discretion as required (Pfeffer and Salancik, 1978).

The that strategic management practices adopted by NPOs in the UK are influenced by external stakeholders and intended to solve problems they expect to meet in their external environments, such as a greater level of competition for donations and, problems in the acquisition of funds (Rehor et al. 2014). Therefore, for NPOs in the UK strategic management practices amount to a combination of management decisions and action plans that these organisations employ to achieve competitive advantage and attain long-term better performance. Strategic management practices potentially reduce organisational weaknesses and leverage their strengths by anticipating prospects and problems.

To this end, it can only be concluded that a majority of the NPOs in the UK have defective strategic management practices – as they are targeted at the external environment, rather than both the internal and external environment. There appears to be a consensus among researchers that the strategic management practices oriented towards both the internal and external environment. This can ensure that NPOs effectively adjust to changing situations in the external or internal environments (Rehor et al. 2014). This will also ensure that NPOs are reaching their specific targets while managing all stakeholder expectations, whether their donors or clients, in a balanced manner.

Result 2: Strategic management models used by NPOs

A majority of participants agreed that their organisations are niche strategists. This implies that they adhere to the specific missions and objectives and do not consider expanding beyond their areas of operation to expand their sources of funds. A majority of the NPOs also appear to use the donor-orientation model, as their focus is on countering competition for donations to appeal to donors. Again, this finding has a theoretical basis in the resource dependence theory, which views these NPOs as focused on attaining ultimate survival depending on their capacity to acquire and maintain resources (Pfeffer and Salancik, 1978, p. 2). NPOs will tend to adopt the donor-orientation model, as it enables them to attain and maintain their funding resources. For this reason, it is understandable that NPOs in the UK will place donors at the center of their operations because of the crucial role they play in sustaining their revenue stream.

There is also a concern that NPOs should pursue a balanced model that emphasizes on both donors and clients, or a model that Weerawardena's *et al.* (2010) suggests that can help the NPOs to 'balance money and mission.' Fundamentally, this model is discussed in the literature as effective owing to its potential to assist organisations to focus on a variety of operational variables like production quality, service quality, production quantity, donor management, and effective budgeting practices.

Result 3: How strategic practices of NPOs differ from those of for-profit organisations

A majority of the participants said that their organisation's strategic management practices differ from those of for-profit organisations, as they mostly aim to attain greater production quantity, reduced expenses, and quality service with the view to appeal to more donations. This idea can be explained by the resource dependence theory, which hypothesizes that an organisation's management practices and decision-making depend on the degree of its resource dependencies (Hillman *et al.* 2009). In other words, external factors like donors are always bound to influence the strategies and decisions of NPOs. Using this perspective, it could be reasoned as for-profit organisations are driven by a need to make more profits and increase their shareholder's wealth, as they depend on shareholders for capital resources. Hence, NPOs and for-profit organisations are bound to have differing strategic management practices. This variation also explains the different levels of efficiency between NPOs and for-profit organisations. It can be reasoned on account of the principal–agency theory, that for-profit organisations tend to be more efficient than NPOs, as for-profit organisations are driven to make profits and increase shareholders' returns (Reeves and Ford 2004). This also demonstrates that a market-oriented mindset has advantages over donor-oriented mindsets in terms of encouraging efficiency in profit-driven business firms. It encourages organisations to design the most suitable services to the target clients and can enable sustainable competitive advantage by encouraging organisations to create superior customer value and better organisational performance (Othman *et al.* 2014).

Result 4: Effects of NPO's external environmental and internal context on strategy formation processes

All participants agreed that the external environmental and internal environment influences the strategy formation processes and the strategies that their organisations use. Consistent with the resource-dependency theory and NPOs' dependence on donors, these organisations continually realise a need to develop new missions while seeking to appeal to a new base of donors. Due to slow funding, NPOs whose missions cannot capture the appeal of donors have to change their missions (Othman *et al.* 2014).

Regarding an organisation's internal environment, it becomes apparent that an effective reward system influences the implementation of a strategic plan, by improving the employee and managers' level of performance in terms of implementing the plan. At the same time, organisation resources and structure play a crucial role in influencing the outcome of a strategic plan. It becomes discernible that when an organisation's resources are not used to the advantage of an organisation, it is possible that the resources are likely to become a waste, which hampers effective development and implementation of a strategic plan. Similarly, when an NPO has robust resources, such as information systems and finances, it is likely to have an effective strategic plan. It is also clear that finances also determine the effectiveness of strategic plans, including by affecting how other resources, like labor or advertising can be procured to implement a plan.

Regarding the external environment, competition for donors and skilled labor influence how NPOs generate and carry out their strategic plans. NPOs seem to consider it proper to engage in strategic management to respond to a need for transparency and accountability by their donors.

It is also clear a strategy formation process plays a role in determining the goals and mission of a strategic plan. It emerges as an indispensable tool for NPOs, as it permits them first do a thorough assessment of their external and internal environments, to acquire information that can guide their strategic planning. It also enables NPOs to focus their activities for strategic planning on the mission and measures of performance, as well as in creating mission, vision, and value that should guide strategic planning.

Alternatively, there is also an agreement among participants and researchers that adopting resource-based strategies would allow NPOs to find and manage all forms of resources, including funding and labor resources, in a fairly balanced manner. This appears to be the case in the UK, whereby NPOs must seek ways to efficiently manage their resources efficiently to improve their performance in an increasingly complex internal and external environment. These organisations should aim to achieve a balance between addressing their external and internal environmental problems, as part of their long-term strategy.

Result 5: Organisational response to changes in the internal and external environment

All seven participants mentioned that they rely on strategic planning to set up strategies to respond to shifts in the internal and external environment. While there appears to be an agreement on the use of strategic planning by the response, the types and focus vary, as a majority of the strategies targeted at the external environment.

Regarding the response to changes in the external environment, strategic planning is an ongoing process in NPOs, that is used to improve quality services to the beneficiaries or target population continually, and to show the donors, funders, and community some positive effects of their services. NPOs also respond through capacity building, such as by building effective teams and creating frameworks that can ensure effective performance to ensure a lasting appeal to donors.

On the other hand, NPOs respond to changes in the internal environment by sometimes delaying strategic planning, due to cash flow challenges, or inability to access the suitable human resource to undertake a strategic plan. This appears to be common among NPOs that lack sufficient funds to implement their strategies and may be a risk management technique an organisation uses from experiencing financial challenges.

Their strategies are intended to ensure the continuous process of improving and evaluating organisational performance. In strategic planning literature, there appears to be a consensus that NPOs should consider integrating CQPI to continually adapt to the shifts in their external and internal environments. It is well supported in current literature that organisations should focus their strategic planning on their external and internal environments, rather than exclusively the internal or external environment (Pecora and Seelig 2001; Giffords and Dina 2004). Use of CQPI by UK NPOs would imply that these organisations engage in planning, goal-setting, and periodic assessments to bring enabled improved performance to the benefit of the organisation and its stakeholders.

Result 6: Reasons for strategic management by NPOs

A majority of participants contend that their organisations are motivated to engage in strategic management in competing for donations. There is also an agreement among researchers that they take on strategic management to collaborate with stakeholders and other organisations and to ensure transparency and accountability by their donors. Current literature supports these findings, and that these translate to a drive-by NPOs to take on strategic management to respond to their external and internal environments.

These views are supported in the previous literature, and an agreement among researchers that NPOs often adopt strategic management practices to manage their internal and external resources adequately. It appears that taking on strategic management to attract donors forms the rationale for NPOs to engage in strategic management. Guided by the resource-dependence theory, NPOs will accommodate strategic practices depending on the degree of the resource dependencies on certain stakeholders. In other words, their strategies are mostly focused on attracting donors, as they depend on them for financial resources. Strategic management enables these organisations to respond to situational issues in an organisation, whereby addressing their financial resources is merely one of those issues (Bryson 2010).

6.0 Conclusion

The research aimed to explore the strategic management practices in NPOs operating in the UK. NPOs in the UK find it difficult gaining absolute control over the affairs and the environment in which their organisations operate in the twenty-first century. They have either failed to, or have been slow to adopt strategic management best practices. There appears to be a need for NPOs to think strategically and to carry out strategic management that can bring about positive outcomes on their performance. Some NPOs are attempting to run their organisations as business enterprises to contend with the competition for funding. Hence, they must invest in enhancing their professional competences using strategic planning.

There comes a question regarding the need to locate suitable methods that can permit NPOs to resolve some fundamental issues regarding their purposes, such as what they are attempting to attain in addition to how they establish and attain their goals and missions. For this reason, some NPOs are seen to have considered it appropriate to engage in strategic management to respond to a need for transparency and accountability by their donors. This shows how strategic planning is becoming indispensable for modern NPOs that want to have sustainable funding options.

It is established in this research that external stakeholders and environmental factors influence strategic management practices that NPOs in the UK employ. The practices are mainly designed to solve problems expected in the external environments. On top of these problems include a greater level of competition for donations and problems in the acquisition of funds. This illustrates that NPOs in the UK have defective strategic management practices targeted at external environment, other than both the internal and external environment. It is recommended that NPOs in the UK must seek ways to efficiently manage their resources efficiently to improve their performance in an increasingly complex internal and external environment. These organisations should aim to achieve a balance between addressing their external and internal environmental problems, as part of their long-term strategy. NPOs in the UK should pursue a balanced model that emphasizes both donors and clients, or a model potentially enables them to 'balance money and mission.'

The research has added knowledge on the significance of having strategic management practices designed to achieve a balance between addressing NPOs external and internal environmental problems. This model is found to be effective as it enables these organisations to focus on a wide variety of operational variables like production quality, service quality, production quantity, donor management, and effective budgeting practices. This can be explained by the resource dependence theory: NPOs' strategic management practices differ from those of for-profit organisations, as they mostly aim to attain greater production quantity, reduced expenses, and quality service with the view to appeal to donations. Regarding the principal–agency theory, it is established that for-profit organisations tend to be efficient than nonprofit organisations as for-profit organisations are driven to make profits and increase shareholders' returns. This also demonstrates that a market-oriented mindset has advantages over donor-oriented mindsets in terms of encouraging efficiency in profit-driven business firms. It encourages organisations to design the most suitable services to the target clients and can enable sustainable competitive advantage by encouraging organisations to create superior customer value and better organisational performance.

This research has some limitations: as the study sample was fairly small, the study results have a narrow capacity for generalisability. Also, the participants were interviewed within a small timeframe depending on their accessibility. This was detrimental as it restricted the number of respondents who the researcher could access. Although a few participants were approached, they are assumed to be a representative of a broad cross-section of perspectives of the managers and leaders of NPOs. Another limitation is related to the sampling method: the convenience sampling used had some drawbacks. Due to its non-random nature, the sample selected may be assumed as not representing the entire target population of UK NPOs that the study focused on.

7.0 Summary

Research aims and objectives: Drawing on a resource dependence conceptual framework to explore the strategic management practices in Non Profit Organisations (NPOs) operating in the UK.

Research methods: The study used interpretivist philosophy as a research approach. Consistent with the inductive approach, a qualitative case study research method was used. Secondary data was collected using document analysis, while Primary data was collected using semi-structured interviews. This was employed to collect participant's perspectives, in turn, complimenting the information generated from a critical review of the literature through document analysis.

Research findings: The study established that None Profit Organisations (NPOs) in the UK have defective strategic management practices that target the external environment, rather than both the internal and external environment. The practices are mainly designed to solve problems expected in the external environment.

Recommendations: NPOs in the UK should aim to address their external and internal environmental problems, as part of their long-term strategy. NPOs in the UK should also pursue a balanced model that emphasises both donors and clients, or a hybrid between a market-oriented and donor-oriented model that would potentially enable them to, what is commonly described in business as 'balance money and mission' .

References

Acevo (2017) *Charity today 2017.* Weblog. [online] Available at: https://www.acevo.org.uk/sites/default/files/%E2%80%98Charity%20Today%20%E2%80%93%202017%E2%80%99%20%E2%80%93%20Briefing%20and%20Stats%20FINAL.pdf (Accessed 27 Jan 2018).

Analoui, F. and Samour, A. (2012). Strategic management: the case of NPOs in Palestine. *Management Research Review,* 35(6), 473-489.

Anheier, H. (2000) Managing non-profit organisations: Towards a new approach. *Civil Society Working Paper 1.*

Bryman, A. (2008) Social Research Methods, Third edn. New York: Oxford University Press.

Bryson, J. M. (2004) *Strategic planning for public and nonprofit organisations: a guide to strengthening and sustaining organisational achievement.* Jossey-Bass, Hoboken, NJ.

Bryson, J. M. (2010) The future of public and nonprofit strategic planning in the United States. *Public Administration Review,* 255-263.

Bryson, J. M., and Alsto, F. K. (2011) *Creating your own strategic plan: A workbook for public and nonprofit organisations.* San Francisco, Jossey-Bass.

Creswell, J. (1998) *Qualitative inquiry and research design: Choosing among five traditions.* SAGE Publications, Thousand Oaks, CA.

Creswell, J. (2002) *Educational research: Planning, conducting, and evaluating quantitative and qualitative research.* Merrill Prentice Hall, Upper Saddle River, NJ.

Elgot, J. (2015) Kids Company: Camila Batmanghelidjh's charity to close amid financial concerns. The Guardian. Weblog. [online] Available at: <https://www.theguardian.com/society/2015/aug/05/childrens-charity-kids-company-close-financial-concerns (Accessed 27 Jan 2018).

Ettner, S. and Hermann, R. (2001) The Role of Profit Status under Imperfect Information: Evidence from the Treatment Patterns of Elderly Medicare Beneficiaries Hospitalised for Psychiatric Diagnoses. || *Journal of Health Economics,* 20(1), 23–49.

Flick, U. (2014) *An introduction to qualitative research,* (5th ed). Los Angeles: SAGE Publications.

Giffords, E. and Dina, R. (2004) Strategic planning in nonprofit organisations: continuous quality performance improvement – a case study. *International Journal of Organisation Theory and Behavior,* 6(4), 66-80.

Guest, G., MacQueen, K.M. and Namey, E.E.. (2011) *Applied thematic analysis.* Thousand Oaks, CA: Sage Publishers

Hecht, B. and Ramsey, R. (2002) *Managing nonprofits.org: Dynamic management for the digital age.* New York, John Wiley and Sons.

Hillman, A., Withers, M. and Collins, B. (2009) Resource dependence theory: A review. *Journal of Management,* 35(6), 1404–1427.

Holatova, R. and Dolesalova, V. (2014) Strategic management methods in non-profit making organisation. *International Journal of Economics and Management Engineering,* 8(9), 3056-60.

Hoonakkera, P., Carayom. P. and Loushine, T. (2010) Barriers and benefits of quality management in the construction industry: An empirical study. *Total Quality Management,* 21(9), 953–969.

Kohli, A. K., and Jaworski, B. (1990) Market orientation: The construct, research propositions and managerial implications. *Journal of Marketing,* 54, 1–18.

Macedo, I. and Pinho, J. (2004) The relationship between resource dependence and market orientation. *European Journal of Marketing,* 40(5), 533-553.

Mair, J., and Marti, I. (2006) Social entrepreneurship research: A source of explanation, prediction, and delight. *Journal of World Business* 41, 36–44.

Mariotto, F., Sanni, P., Salati, G. (2012) What is the use of a single-case study in management research?. *Revista de Administração de Empresas,* 4(4), 358-369.

Mason, J. (2002) Qualitative Researching, 2nd edn. Thousand Oaks, CA: Sage Publications.

McLeod, S. (2017) Qualitative vs. quantitative. *Simply Psychology.* [Online] Available at: https://www.simplypsychology.org/qualitative-quantitative.html (Accessed 21 Oct 2018)

Miles, M. and Huberman, M. (1994) *Qualitative data analysis: an expanded source book.* Newbury Park, Sage.

Mort, G., and Weerawardena, J. (2008) Social entrepreneurship: Advancing research and maintaining relevance. In A. Sargeant and W. Wymer (Eds.), *The Routledge companion to nonprofit marketing* (pp. 28–48). London: Routledge.

Mulhare, E. (1999) Mindful of the Future: Strategic planning ideology and the culture of nonprofit management. *Human Organisation,* 323-330

Mulhare, E. (1999) Mindful of the Future: Strategic planning ideology and the culture of nonprofit management. *Human Organisation,* 323-330.

Ogonji , M. (2014) *Strategic planning in nonprofit organisations: a content analysis of best practices.* Trinity Washington University.

Onwuegbusie, A, Leech, N and Collins, K. (2012) Qualitative analysis techniques for the review of the literature. *The Qualitative Report* 17(56), 1-28

Pecora, P., and Seelig, W.R. (1997) The changing world of service for children and families in quality improvement and evaluation. In Pecora, P. J., Seeling, W. R., Sirps, F. A. and Davis, S. M. (Eds.), *Child and Family Services: Managing into the Next Century* (pp. 5-25). Washington, CWLA Press.

Peredo, A. and McLean, M. (2006) Social entrepreneurship: A critical review of the concept. *Journal of World Business,* 41, 56–65.

Pfeffer, J., and Salancik, G. R. (1978) *The external control of organisations: A resource dependence perspective.* New York, HarperCollins.

Reeves, T. C. and Ford, E. W. (2004) Strategic Management and Performance Differences: Nonprofit versus For-Profit Health Care Organisations. *Health Care Management Review,* 29(4), 298-308.

Rehor, P., Holátova, D. and Doležalova, V. (2014) Strategic management methods in non-profit making organisation. *International Journal of Economics and Management Engineering,* 8(9), 3056-3060.

Saunders, M., Lewis, P., Thornhill, A. (2016) *Research methods for business students.* 7th edition. Essex, Pearson Education Limited.

Seelos, C., and Mair, J. (2005) Entrepreneurs in service of the poor—Models for business contributions to sustainable development. *Business Horisons,* 48(3), 241–246.

The Guardian (2015) *Kids Company let down by its trustees.* Weblog. [online] Available at: https://www.theguardian.com/society/2015/aug/11/kids-company-let-down-by-its-trustees (Accessed 27 Jan 2018).

Thomas, J. and Harden, A. (2008) Methods for the thematic synthesis of qualitative research in systematic reviews. *BMC Med Res Methodol,* v 8(45), 1.

Valentinov, V. (2008) The economics of nonprofit organisation: In search of an integrative theory. *Journal of Economic Issues* 17(3), 745–761.

Verbruggen, H, Christiaens, J and Milis, K 2009, "Can resource dependence explain not-for-profit organisation's compliance with reporting standards?," *HUB Research Paper 2009/24.*

Weerasooriya, W. and Khatibi, A. and Alwis, A. (2014) The impact of strategic planning for non-government organisations in Sri Lanka: an evaluation using the balanced scorecard – development of a conceptual framework. *International Journal of Arts and Commerce,* 3(4), 35-48.

Weerawardena, J. and Mort, G. (2012) Competitive strategy in socially entrepreneurial nonprofit organisations: Innovation and differentiation. *Journal of Public Policy and Marketing,* 31(1), 91–101.

Weerawardena, J., McDonald, R. and Mort, G. (2010) Sustainability of nonprofit organisations: An empirical investigation. *Journal of World Business,* 45, 346–356.

Wilbur, R. H. (2000) *The Complete Guide to Nonprofit Management* (2nd ed.). New York, John Wiley and Sons.

Williams, C. (2007) Research methods. *Journal of Business and Economic Research,* 5(3), 65-71.

Wilson, W. and Chaddha, A. 2010. The role of theory in ethnographic research. *Ethnography,* 10(4), pp.549-564

Yin, R. (1984) *Case study research: design and methods.* London, Sage Publications.

Appendices

Appendix 1: Consent form.

Consent Form for Holly Parrott MBA project: Title of the study: An Overview of The Strategic Management Practices in NPOs- Case Study UK

- I confirm that I have read and understood the information sheet for the above project and the researcher has answered any queries to my satisfaction.
- I understand that my participation is voluntary and that I am free to withdraw from the project at any time, up to the point of completion, without having to give a reason and without any consequences. If I exercise my right to withdraw and I don't want my data to be used, any data which have been collected from me will be destroyed.
- I understand that any identifiable information relating to myself or the organisation that I represent will be withdrawn from the study.
- I understand that any information recorded in the investigation will remain confidential and secure and no information that identifies me will be made to any other parties, except the researcher.
- I consent to be a participant in the project
- I consent to being audio recorded as part of the project

(PRINT NAME)

Signature of Participant:

Date:

Appendix 2 Participant information sheet

Participant Information Sheet for Holly Parrott MBA project: Title of the research: An Overview of The Strategic Management Practices in NPOs- Case Study UK

Introduction

My name is Holly Parrott and I am a currently study a MBA at the University of the West of Scotland. I am on my final dissertation for my MBA and thank you for considering contributing to my research. I can be contacted by email B00319903@studentmail.uws.ac.uk or mobile 079294649987.

What is the purpose of this investigation?

I believe that current management and organisational research have not adequately addressed the question of strategic management of NPOs in the UK, and whether they should be managed distinctly from the profit-driven business firm and whether they should be managed using different management practices and models. The aim of my research is to:

- Explore the strategic management practices used by NPOs in the UK;

- Investigate the strategic management models used by NPOs;
- Determine how strategic practices of NPOs differ from those of for-profit organisations;
- Examine the effects of NPO's external environmental and internal context on strategy formation processes;
- Investigate how Organisations in the UK respond to changes in the internal and external environment;
- Determine the reasons for strategic management by NPOs in the UK.

Do you have to take part?

No, participation is completely voluntary and will take no more than an hour of your time and all information will be treated in the strictest of confidence. For that reason, I am happy to meet you at a convenient time at your place of work, or via Skype. The conversation will be orientated around some broad questions, but should be quite relaxed throughout and I will use a voice recorder to make notes, so you do not appear on camera, and I can ensure that I review things accurately at a later date.

Why have you been invited to take part?

- I have been careful in who I have asked to assist me in my research and the key factors that have helped me in this selection is that the participants and the organisations they represent are:
- Organised and possess certain institutional realities- such as having an organised system of governance, policies, strategic plans, workplace policies and defined organisations behaviours
- Are private and tend to be institutionally distinct from government;
- Are non-profit-distributing and do not return any profit they make to donors or owners
- Are intrinsically voluntary and participating is not compulsory;
- Have reported steady growth in the last decade.

What are the potential risks to you in taking part?

I will require the most of an hour of your day: all information gathered will be kept on a secure system that is password protected, has the latest protection software and will not be access by any other individual other than myself. When writing my dissertation, all personal details and any specifics mentioned will be removed to ensure that both you and your organisations are protected.

Thank you for reading this information – please ask any questions if you are unsure about what is written here.

What happens next?

If you are happy to be involved in the project, I will send you a consent form to sign, and then we can arrange a confident time to meet/Skype.

If you do not want to be involved in the project, I can understand and thank you for your consideration.

If you have any questions/concerns, during or after the investigation, please do not hesitate to contact me further.

Printed in Great Britain
by Amazon